The Eigh

The Eighties

Photographs by the
Daily Mail

Duncan Hill

This is a Parragon Book
First published in 2003

Parragon
Queen Street House
4 Queen Street
Bath, BA1 1HE, UK

Text © Parragon
All photographs © Associated Newspapers Archive

Produced by Atlantic Publishing

A catalogue record for this book is available from the British Library.
ISBN 0 75259 028 6

Printed in China

The Eighties

Margaret Thatcher declared there was no such thing as society. The decade became synonymous with acquisitiveness, and "yuppy" entered the language. Unemployment soared, and places like Toxteth and Brixton saw the worst civil unrest for generations.

The Gang of Four set up the SDP, while a rather larger gang set up camp at Greenham Common to protest over cruise missiles.

The miners tested the Government's resolve, and Argentina invaded the Falklands. Both found that the lady was not for turning.

There were many disasters: Zeebrugge, Piper Alpha, King's Cross, Lockerbie. Britain was battered by hurricane-force winds - after Michael Fish told us not to worry.

Sport also had its share of tragedy, at Heysel, Hillsborough and Bradford. But Torvill and Dean enthralled us, while millions stayed up to watch Dennis Taylor win on that final black.

There were street parties as Charles and Diana tied the knot. Live Aid was a worldwide party, as Bob Geldof pricked the world's conscience over the starving of Ethiopia.

From the momentous and the apocalyptic to the offbeat and the trivial, the photographs in this book, from the archives of the *Daily Mail*, chart the people, places and events that made up a memorable decade.

The Eighties

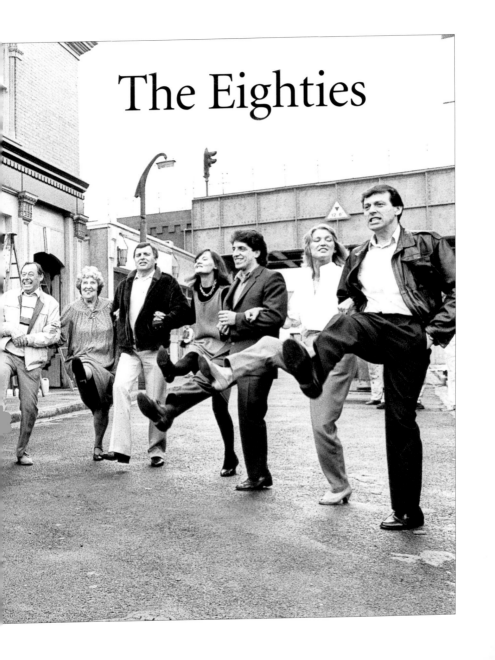

Iranian embassy siege

Iranian demonstrators praying in London the day after terrorists had seized control of the Iranian embassy in London demanding the release of political prisoners in Iran following the Iranian Revolution the previous year.

Opposite: The burnt-out Iranian embassy building on 6 May 1980, the day after the SAS had stormed the building and ended the siege, which had begun on 30 April.

Previous pages: The cast of *EastEnders* prematurely celebrating the success of the new show.

'Growing friendship' with Prince Charles

The press first began to realise a growing friendship was developing between Lady Diana Spencer and Prince Charles in the autumn of 1980. After she was invited to holiday with Prince Charles and the royal family at Balmoral, Diana returned to London to find photographers camped on her doorstep and at the kindergarten where she worked. She was no stranger to the royal family, her first home being Park House in the grounds of Sandringham. Her maternal grandparents had been great friends of King George VI and the Queen Mother and some of her childhood playmates were Prince Andrew and Prince Edward.

Opposite: Swedish tennis player Bjorn Borg celebrates his fifth successive Wimbledon triumph after beating John McEnroe in a dramatic four-hour, five set final.

Botham and Coe

England cricketer Ian Botham meets West Indies captain Clive Lloyd for tea. Botham was to help England win the Ashes the following year in 1981, and he was to go on to represent his country 102 times before retirement.

Opposite: Sebastian Coe training for the Moscow Olympics. Coe went on to win gold in the 1500 metres and silver in the 800 metres behind his team-mate Steve Ovett. Coe repeated his success at the Olympics in Los Angeles four years later but was deemed unfit for selection for the Seoul 1988 team. He retired from athletics in 1990 and became a Conservative MP in 1992.

New Labour leader

Michael Foot at Labour Party headquarters on his first day as Labour Party leader. His celebration was short-lived as he had to defend his stance against Britain possessing nuclear weapons to Margaret Thatcher in the Commons, pulling Labour away from a common defence policy it had shared with the Conservatives in the 1970s.

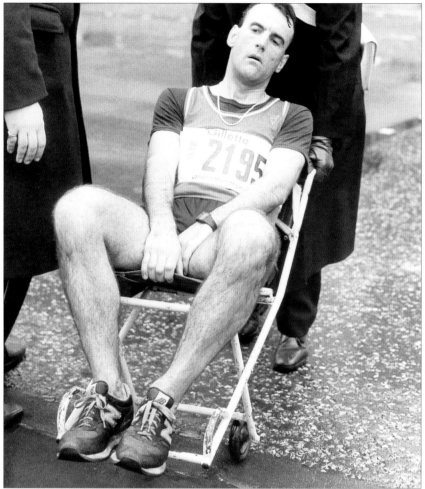

First London Marathon

The first-ever London Marathon saw 6700 competitors running the 26 miles 385 yards from
Greenwich Park to Buckingham Palace.
Winners Inge Simonsen of Norway and Dick Beardsley of the United States crossed the finish line
together in 2 hours, 11 minutes and 48 seconds. They pose, garlanded (*opposite*), with Joyce Smith
the first woman home.

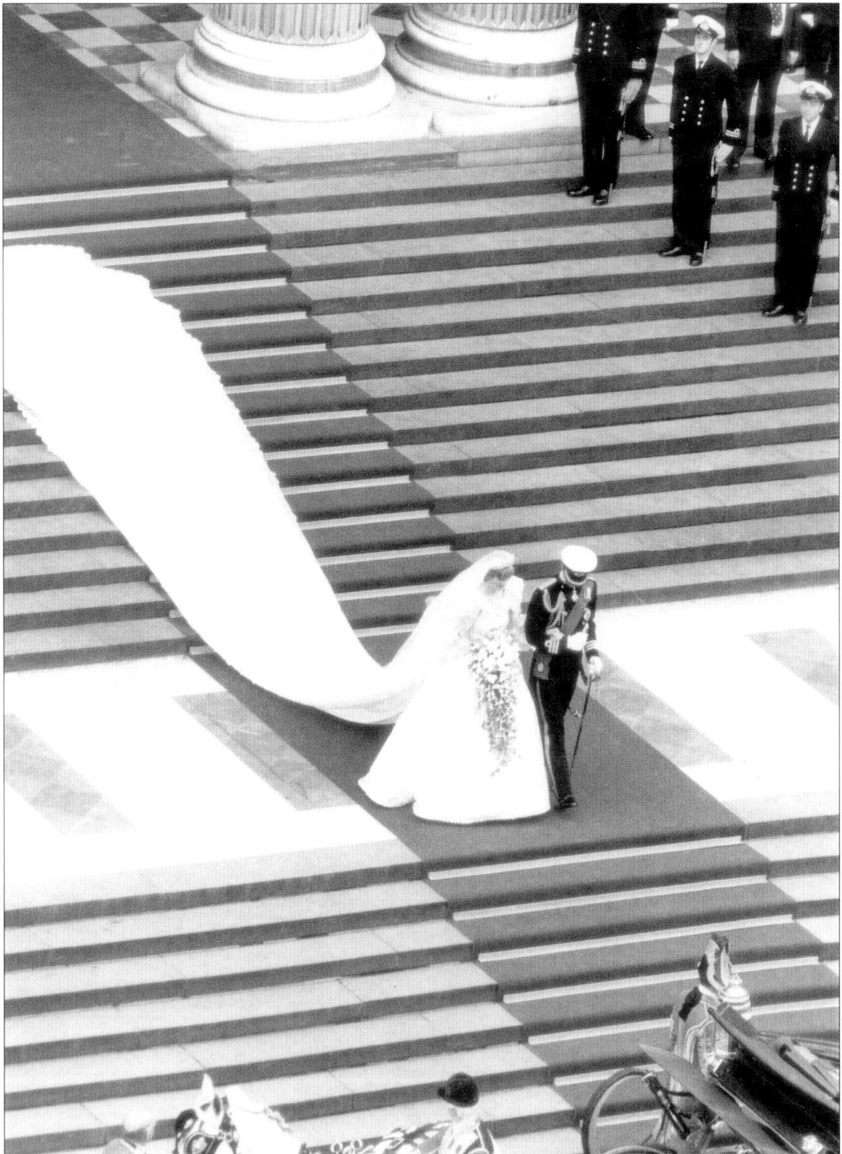

700 million watch Royal Wedding

The Prince and Princess of Wales leaving St Paul's and on the balcony of Buckingham Palace shortly after their wedding ceremony on 29 July 1981. 700 million viewers across the world watched the marriage on television.

Golden boys

Britain's Allan Wells, Sebastian Coe and Daley Thompson make their first track appearance since winning gold medals at the Moscow Olympics at the IAC Coca-Cola Athletics Championship at Crystal Palace. The US boycott of the Olympics was in part responsible for Britain's increased success in the competition.

Opposite: Tennis stars John Lloyd and Chris Evert at Surbiton when they were married.

New Romantics

The Eighties reaction to punk was the theatrical clothes, extravagant hairdos and make-up of the
New Romantics. Bands like Duran Duran, Spandau Ballet, Soft Cell, Human League and Depeche
Mode led the way on the music front.

Botham and Willis inspire England

In one of the most amazing comebacks in Test history, England recovered from a near innings defeat to beat Australia by 18 runs. Ian Botham scored 149 to give England a chance and with Australia still only needing 130 runs to win Bob Willis took 8 wickets for 43 runs to secure victory.

Opposite: Labour's Ken Livingstone visited protesters at London County Hall in July 1981 who were demonstrating for the release of IRA prisoners on hunger strikes at the Maze prison in demand for Prisoner of War status for IRA prisoners within all Ulster jails.

Anwar Sadat assassinated

The funeral procession of Egyptian President Anwar Sadat moves through the streets of Cairo after he was assassinated by Islamic fundamentalists due in part to his peace treaty with Israel which outraged the Arab world. Vice-President Hosni Mubarak assumed control of the country upon Sadat's death.

Opposite: Denis Healey working on his speech for the Labour Party Conference on the beach at Brighton, where the event was to take place. Healey had just been re-elected as deputy leader of the Labour party.

The Falklands War

The Argentine army stands to attention as the Argentine flag is hoisted up the flagpole (with some difficulty) outside Government House in Port Stanley following the Argentine invasion of the Falkland Islands. The leader of the Argentinian dictatorship, Galtieri invaded the islands in order to unite the people behind a military success and shift attention away from the domestic economic and employment concerns.

Opposite: Survivors being helped onshore at Blue Cove, East Falklands after two British landing ships the *Sir Galahad* and the *Sir Tristram* suffered air attacks. One week later the Argentinian forces surrendered Port Stanley, ending the Falklands War in which 255 Britons and 652 Argentines died.

Solidarity in Poland

Gdansk shipyard worker, Lech Walesa, the founder of the independent trade union movement, Solidarity, arrives at Heathrow Airport following his release from prison in his native Poland. He was arrested in 1981 when the Polish authorities declared martial law and clamped down upon dissenting political movements. Two years later, in 1983, he won the Nobel Peace Prize. After the Polish constitution was amended in 1990 to allow freer elections he won a landslide victory and became the President of Poland for five years.

Opposite: The height of early eighties New Romantic fashion in its full extravagance.

The Gang of Four

David Owen, William Rodgers, Shirley Williams and Roy Jenkins were thrown out of the Labour
Party for forming a Council for Social Democracy and later forming the Social Democratic Party.
The 'Gang of Four' as they became known criticised Labour for drifting towards extremism and
called for a classless struggle for social justice.

Opposite: Police surrounding skinheads after 400 of them went on a rampage in Southend-on-Sea
and other seaside resorts. Police rounded up 250 troublemakers in Southend alone and sent them
home on a specially policed train.

Welcome Prince William

Prince William was born on June 21 1982, at St Mary's Hospital in Paddington, London.
He weighed in at 7lb 1oz and was born after a 16-hour labour. It had been a very public pregnancy with much written in the press. Following the wishes of his parents he was born in hospital rather than in Buckingham Palace. It was another seven days before his name was officially announced as William Arthur Philip Louis.

Manchester United and Liverpool in Wembley Final

Bob Paisley leads the Liverpool squad on to the pitch at Wembley alongside Ron Atkinson, manager of Manchester United. The two sides were about to play one another in the League Cup Final which Liverpool were to win in what was to be Paisley's final season at the club. Also in view are captains Ray Wilkins and Graeme Souness.

Opposite: Guests leave the funeral of Princess Grace of Monaco, after she died tragically, aged 52, when the car she was in plummeted 120 feet off a mountain road. Her daughter Princess Stephanie was alongside her. She gave up Hollywood when she married Prince Rainer III in 1956. Her last film was *High Society* made in the same year as her wedding.

Fourteen-mile chain around Greenham Common

In April 1983, Campaign for Nuclear Disarmament supporters formed a human chain that linked Burghfield, Aldermaston and Greenham. The protest was peaceful and no arrests were made. The defence Secretary called the CND marchers 'naive'.

Chairman Elton

Opposite: Under the watchful eye of Chairman Mao a deal is struck. Graham Taylor and Elton John meet outside Mao's tomb in Beijing after Watford FC had played three matches in China during the summer. The club which Taylor managed and of which Elton John was chairman reached second position in the League to Liverpool in the 1982-3 season.
Above: Labour leader Michael Foot meets stars of the stage and screen who support Labour including Maureen Lipman, Colin Welland and Larry Adler.

Kinnock leader of the opposition

Outgoing Labour Party leader Michael Foot and his wife Jill Craigie acknowledge a standing ovation which preceded his final parliamentary report as party leader to the party's Brighton conference. Neil Kinnock, who replaced Foot, gives a speech at the same conference.

Street star to marry

Coronation Street actress Pat Phoenix who played Elsie Tanner walks with actor Anthony Booth. The pair would marry three years later in September 1986.

Opposite: Chris Evert Lloyd is beaten by Kathy Jordan in the women's singles tournament at Wimbledon although she would go on to win both the Australian and French Opens that same year.

Daley's rival

Great Britain's Daley Thompson playfully warns his greatest rival Jurgen Hingsen of Germany at a chance passing in Lanzarote ahead of their meeting in the decathlon of the 1984 Olympic Games in Los Angeles. Thompson went on to win his second consecutive gold, setting a new Olympic record.

Torvill and Dean's bolero

Opposite: All nine judges gave maximum points for artistic merit to Jayne Torvill and Christopher Dean as they skated to gold in the Winter Olympics in February 1984. It was a poignant Valentine's Day for the Nottingham pair who skated to the rhythm of Ravel's *Bolero*.

Above: Beatlemania makes a return to Liverpool, when Paul goes back to attend the British première of *Give My Regards to Broad Street* at the Odeon Cinema, and to collect a gold-framed scroll honouring him as a Freeman of the City. All of the Beatles had been made Freemen the previous year, but Paul is the first to come in person to receive the honour. Linda receives a silver salver in the same ceremony, held in Lime Street's Picton Library.

Lawson's budget

Opposite: The Chancellor of the Exchequer, the Right Honourable Nigel Lawson MP works on his presentation in preparation for the Budget the following week on March 13 1984.
Above: David Bowie leaving Jerry Hall's 27th birthday party celebrations in London. The following year Bowie collaborated with Mick Jagger on the single and video release 'Dancing In The Street' for Live Aid.

Lauda's third championship

Niki Lauda claims his third win of the 1984 season in the British Grand Prix. His driver's championship victory that year earned him membership of the exclusive club of three-time winners, a club whose only other members were Fangio, Brabham and Stewart.

Opposite: Jerry Hall and Mick Jagger after the birth of their daughter Elizabeth Scarlett at the Berkeley Square Ball London July 1984.

Stewart still wearing it well

Singer Rod Stewart at Heathrow Airport en route from Spain to Los Angeles without his new girlfriend Kelly Emberg. Stewart released 'Infatuation', 'Some Guys Have all the Luck' and 'Alright Now' in the same year.

Opposite: Armed police outside the Libyan Embassy during the siege in which Policewoman Yvonne Fletcher was shot whilst accompanying a demonstration against the embassy apparently being used for terrorist activities. The British government severed links with Colonel Gaddafi's government but allowed the Libyan students and diplomats hiding inside to return home and Fletcher's murderers were never caught.

Breakdancing

Opposite: The 1980s saw breakdancing spreading from New York to the rest of the world due in part to the release of several breakdancing films including *Beat Street* and *Flash Dance* in 1984. The dance style incorporates elements of acrobatics, gymnastics, mime and martial arts.
Above: Jean Alexander plays Hilda Ogden, still going strong in her third decade in *Coronation Street*.

Brighton bomb

Above: Prime Minister Margaret Thatcher dances at a civic reception with Brighton's mayor John Blackman at the Tory Party Conference, unaware of the pending IRA bomb attack upon the hotel of the Tory Cabinet in which the Prime Minister narrowly escaped death. MP Sir Anthony Berry and wife of a chief whip, John Wakehan, were not so lucky.

Opposite: Pop Artist Andy Warhol poses for a photograph in 1984. In the early 1980s Warhol made two cable television series, *Andy Warhol's TV* and *Andy Warhol's Fifteen Minutes* for MTV prior to his death in 1987 during gall bladder surgery.

LONDON BOROUGH OF WALFORD
ALBERT SQUARE
E20

Liverpool's deadly duo

Ian Rush and Kenny Dalglish in celebratory mood. Their strike partnership was the most prolific of the Eighties. After signing for Liverpool in 1980 'Rushie' scored 229 goals in 469 appearances while 'King Kenny' netted 118 times in 355 games.

Opposite: *EastEnders* actresses, Wendy Richard (Left) and Shirley Cheriton, pose in Albert Square, Walford for the launch of the new bi-weekly serial. *EastEnders* remained popular throughout the 1980s and 1990s and continues to top ratings listings in the new millennium.

He comes and goes

Opposite: Boy George quashes rumours that he plans to quit Britain ahead of a Franco-German tour by wearing a Union Jack shirt and dying his hair red, white and blue. Culture Club's record, 'The War Song', was number one across Europe at the time.

Above: Neil Kinnock poses with his Shadow Cabinet which includes the future party leader John Smith the then Shadow Minister for Trade and Industry and future Deputy Prime Minister John Prescott, then Shadow Employment Minister.

Wogan shown the door

Terry Wogan gets a helping hand from two doormen as he leaves the BBC Radio 2 *Morning Show* for the last time. In fact Wogan was to return to the show in 1993.

Opposite: Two victims blinded by the gas leak from the Union Carbide plant in Bhopal, India stand outside the plant after the disaster. 2000 people died in the immediate aftermath and as many as 200,000 more suffered long-term health problems including blindness, liver and kidney failure.

Thriller

Michael Jackson is surrounded by fans outside Madame Tussaud's in London where he viewed his effigy. That year Jackson won the Best Music Video Grammy Award for his song 'Thriller', and teamed up with Lionel Richie, Cindy Lauper and Stevie Wonder to sing 'We are the World', at the American Music Awards which won him a Grammy the following year for Song of 1985.
Opposite: Norman Whiteside holds the FA Cup aloft after scoring the winning goal for Manchester United against Everton in the 110th minute of the 1985 final. The score after 90 minutes was 0-0. Whiteside put an end to Everton's hopes of winning an historic treble.

Terry Waite greets hostages

Terry Waite, the Archbishop of Canterbury's special envoy (*second left*) greets three British hostages, Robin Plummer, Michael Berdinner and Malcolm Anderson at Gatwick Airport after their release from Libya. Waite himself was to become a hostage in Beirut two years later whilst petitioning for the release of more British hostages.

Opposite: 'Yuppies'- Young Upwardly Mobile Persons - want money above all else according to a survey by Agency McCann Erikson. The children of the Thatcher era, as they became known, were criticised for their selfishness.

Street life

The cast of *Coronation Street* celebrate with Jean Alexander as she returns to the street after accepting an award from the Royal Television Society.

Opposite: Robin Cousins poses with his son, Robin Cousins Junior on the ice in August 1985. He has Olympic and European championships gold medals to his name and in 1985 he was achieving back flip-triple toe-loop combinations in practice and by 1986 he famously performed two consecutive layout back flips in competition.

Simon and Yasmin

Duran Duran singer Simon Le Bon poses for photographers with his partner, model Yasmin Parvaneh at the *Elle* magazine launch. The pair married two months later. Duran Duran had hits throughout the 1980s including 'Notorious', 'Rio', and the theme to the James Bond film, *A View to a Kill*.

Opposite: Comedian Lenny Henry accompanied hordes of schoolchildren on a fun run in Battersea Park as part of a YMCA Drugs Prevention appeal. Around 5000 children from schools across London participated in the race.

Band Aid

Boomtown Rats' singer Bob Geldof receives a cheque for £100,000 for the Band Aid campaign from Food Aid's Terry Wogan and poses alongside his wife, Paula Yates at a function promoting his number One hit, 'Don't they know it's Christmas', which raised £5 million for famine sufferers in Ethiopia. In July 1985 Geldof brought together the best of rock and pop for concerts held simultaneously in Wembley and Philadelphia.

Maradona's 'Hand of God'

Glenn Hoddle bursts past Marcel Coras during England's World Cup qualifying match against Romania, which they drew 1-1. England were to reach the quarter-finals at the World Cup in Mexico the following year, where they were beaten 2-1 by Argentina partly due to Maradona's infamous 'Hand-of-God', 54th-minute goal.

Opposite: Bob Geldof, who was given an honorary knighthood in 1986, tours Ethiopia to see how the effects of the Band Aid funds were being felt.

Branson's Virgin take off

Entrepreneur Richard Branson alongside cricketer Ian Botham. By the 1980s Branson's Virgin Records was one of the top six record companies in the world and from June 1984 Branson launched Virgin Airways, a trans-Atlantic jumbo jet flight from London to New York. Subsequently his airline flies to over 21 destinations worldwide.

Opposite: Television personality Anneka Rice poses with comedian Michael Barrymore. Rice became famous through the television series *Treasure Hunt* for which she won the 'Rear of the Year' award. In 1986 she was a presenter on TV-AM and in the late 1980s she would go on to present her own primetime show, *Challenge Anneka*. Barrymore had his own comedy show during the eighties.

M25 motorway completed

Prime Minister Margaret Thatcher on the final completed stretch of the M25 motorway loop around London which she opened in October 1986.

Opposite: Player-manager Kenny Dalglish celebrates his 23rd-minute goal for Liverpool against Chelsea which secured his team the league championship title. Liverpool were ten points adrift of Manchester United by November but managed to turn the tables in the second half of the season by securing 34 points out of a possible 36. In his 12 seasons at Anfield Dalglish won 20 major trophies.

Militant

Neil Kinnock arrives at Labour Party Headquarters for the party's National Executive Committee meeting where he was to interview Militant Tendency members. Militant Tendency was a radical Trotskyite faction which was banned and expelled from the Labour Party shortly after the meeting. *Opposite*: Actress Felicity Kendal poses for the camera to promote her new television series *The Mistress* in which she played opposite Jane Asher and Jack Galloway. Kendal became famous through her role as Barbara Good in the television series *The Good Life*.

BAFTA nominees

An array of actors including David Jason and Nigel Hawthorne line up for a photo once they heard of their nominations for a BAFTA award.

Opposite: Steve Ovett running the 1500m at Crystal Palace in 1986. After starting the decade successfully with a gold medal in the 800m at the Moscow Olympics, 1986 proved to be a turning point in his successes. He only ranked third in the UK in the 1500m although he did manage to win the gold in the 5000m at the Commonwealth Games in Edinburgh.

Rik Mayall: The New Statesman

Rik Mayall poses by a 'For Members Only', sign to promote his latest television series *The New Statesman* a satire in which he plays a Conservative MP. Mayall became famous for his role as Rick in *The Young Ones* in 1982 and would go on to star in cult television series *Bottom* in the early 1990s.

Opposite: *The Herald Of Free Enterprise*, ferry which sank off Zeebrugge, Belgium, in March 1987.

Syrian soldiers in Beirut

Syrian soldiers police West Beirut after Shiite Amal Militia besieged the Shatila Palestinian Refugee Camp and requisitioned supplies. The Syrians helped put an end to the fighting between rival Muslim groups in the Lebanese capital in February, two months before they broke the siege. A local resident shows his appreciation of the Syrian presence.

Madonna: Queen of Pop

The Queen of Pop, Madonna arrives with heavy security at London's Heathrow Airport at the start of a British tour. Madonna shot to the number one spot for six weeks in November 1984 with 'Like a Virgin'. In 1987 she starred in *Who's that Girl?* alongside British actor Sir John Mills.
Opposite: Nigel Mansell wins the British Grand Prix at Silverstone in 1987. It was the British driver's finest hour as he famously passed Nelson Piquet on the 63rd lap of 65 at Stowe Corner.

Third term for Thatcher

Prime Minister Margaret Thatcher and her husband Denis outside 10 Downing Street in June 1987 after returning from Conservative Central Office. Mrs Thatcher is giving the 'three sign' for victory, signifying that she is the only Prime Minister this century to have been elected for a third term.

Opposite: A young supporter celebrates the Premier's third consecutive election victory. The Conservatives took 375 seats to Labour's 229.

SDP and the Liberals

The Social Democrat Roy Jenkins alongside the Liberal leader David Steel at the Liberal Party Conference after they suffered an overwhelming election defeat by the Conservatives in 1987, winning only 22 seats. The Alliance had already crumbled before the votes had been counted as Social Democrats' leader David Owen accused Steel of trying to force the SDP into a Liberal-controlled merger. At the conference the two parties had to discuss closer but fairer integration.

Opposite: Boris Becker hits the ball at Queen's Tennis Club. In 1987 he was to come second at Wimbledon after two consecutive victories in the men's singles tournament in 1985 and 1986. Becker's career lasted well into the nineties but his most successful year was 1989 when he won both Wimbledon and the US Open. His first Wimbledon victory had made him the youngest-ever champion at just seventeen.

Equal rights

Women campaign for equal rights to employment opportunities outside the Labour Party
Conference in Brighton. The banners demand one woman be short-listed for every job opportunity.
Labour used the conference to reappraise their strategy after their election defeat.
Opposite: Model and television presenter Marie Helvin helps promote Harrods exclusive Couture
range of tights and stockings. Helvin released her autobiography *Catwalk, The Art of Model Style* in
1985 in which she combined her own life experiences with practical tips to aspiring models.

Ronald Reagan at Downing Street

US President Ronald Reagan outside 10 Downing Street for talks with Margaret Thatcher following his visit to Moscow. While in London he gave a speech at the Guildhall.

Welcoming Scarlett

Comedian Billy Connolly and fiancée Pamela Stephenson leave the Portland Hospital with their new baby Scarlett. The pair would marry the following year in September 1989.

Opposite: Model and actress Joan Collins taking a break in Marrakech. Collins' career was revived in the 80s when she appeared as Alexis Carrington in the successful TV series *Dynasty*.

Good neighbours, good friends

Actress and singer Kylie Minogue with Jason Donovan. The nineteen-year-olds, who have launched solo singing careers, both star in *Neighbours*, the popular Australian soap.
Opposite: Germany's Boris Becker defeats Ivan Lendl in the Wimbledon semi-finals only to be beaten by the less well-known, Swedish Stefan Edberg in the final. Edberg holds the men's singles trophy aloft. Edberg won by 3 sets to Becker's 1.

Michael and the Prince's Trust

Michael Jackson performs at Wembley Stadium in front of the Prince and Princess of Wales.
He presented Diana, a Jackson fan, with specially engraved CDs of his hit albums *Bad* and *Thriller*
and provided the Prince's Trust with a £150,000 cheque from his tour sponsors Pepsi.

The Rolling Stone

Rolling Stones lead guitarist, Keith Richards, en route to Paris. He was with the band when they released such songs as, 'Satisfaction' and 'Brown Sugar'. But by 1986 a feud with Mick Jagger threatened the future of the Rolling Stones and Richards began to embark on a solo career, releasing 'Don't take it so hard' and later teaming up with the likes of Chuck Berry and Aretha Franklin.
Opposite: America's Carl Lewis warming up at the Van Damme Memorial meeting in the Heysel Stadium in Brussels six months after winning Olympic gold at Seoul for the long jump. Subsequently, he was awarded the gold in the 100 metres after the winner, Ben Johnson, failed a drugs test. Lewis won four golds at Los Angeles in 1984 and went on to win his third consecutive long jump gold at Barcelona in 1992.

Looking forward

Conservative Party Chairman Peter Brooke and Brighton Mayoress Pat Hawkes alongside Prime Minister Margaret Thatcher at the Tory Party Conference in Brighton. Unlike the banner predicts, Margaret Thatcher would not lead the country for very far into the new decade; she was ousted by her own party in 1990.

Opposite: Bono and The Edge of Irish rock group U2. The band achieved their first UK number one in 1988 for their song 'Desire'. *Rattle and Hum* gave U2 a number one album in the same year.

Ben's first novel

Author and comedian Ben Elton promotes his first novel, *Stark*. It would be reprinted 23 times in its first year of publication alone. Elton made his name through writing or creating television mini-series including *Mr Bean* and *Blackadder*, which was in its fourth series in 1989.
Opposite: On Christmas Day Prince William accompanies his cousin Zara Phillips after the traditional morning service at Sandringham.

Tyson, Bruno and Naomi

Mike Tyson and Frank Bruno in a friendly off-duty moment. Things weren't so amicable in February
1989 when the two stepped into the ring in Las Vegas. Tyson recovered from a Bruno onslaught in
the first round to finish the contest with a ferocious barrage in the fifth. Tyson had become the
youngest world heavyweight boxing champion in November 1986 with awesome punching power
and speed not seen since Muhammad Ali.

Opposite: Naomi Campbell struts on the catwalk; the eighteen-year-old was talent-spotted by Mike
Tyson after the title fight with Frank Bruno and shot to fame. It was estimated that she earned over
£1 million in 1989 alone.

Wax on wheels

Ruby Wax walks arm in arm with Lady Killearn, the subject of the first episode of Wax's new television show, *Wax on Wheels*. The series followed the success of Wax's 1988 show, *Ruby's Celebrity Bash* and led to her production of *East Meets Wax* in 1989, which saw the comedienne tour Communist Russia.

Opposite: Prince Harry attends the Easter Sunday service at St George's Chapel, Windsor Castle with his mother.

Perestroika

Mikhail Gorbachev poses for the press outside 10 Downing Street and makes a speech at the Guildhall during his visit to London. Gorbachev also visited the Pope in the same year in a string of attempts at rapprochement with the West following his domestic policies of Glasnost and Perestroika. But time was running out for Gorbachev. His leadership was already being challenged as Boris Yeltsin had already won an astounding 89% of the votes in the first multi-candidate elections for the Congress of People's Deputies.

Hillsborough tragedy

Tributes are paid by both the public and the Prime Minister in the wake of the Hillsborough
disaster where 95 people were killed when they were crushed in the West Stand of Sheffield
Wednesday's ground, which was overfilled by an influx of supporters eager to see the FA Cup semi
final tie between Liverpool and Nottingham Forest.

The special relationship

President George Bush outside 10 Downing Street with Margaret Thatcher and with his wife Barbara as they board Air Force One. It was Bush's first visit to Britain as President and he put particular emphasis on the 'special relationship' between the two countries. Bush and Thatcher discussed the need to shift their policy regarding the Soviet Union from military confrontation to an attempt at economic integration, in the wake of Gorbachev's reforms.

The Foreign Secretary

Foreign Secretary John Major stands outside the Foreign and Commonwealth Office
shortly before he was to become Chancellor of the Exchequer in a Cabinet reshuffle. He was not
Chancellor for long as he rose to party leader and thus Prime Minister upon Margaret Thatcher's
exit in 1990 until his landslide defeat in 1997.
Opposite: Mick Jagger struts his stuff on stage during the Rolling Stones 'Steel Wheels' world tour.
The album of the same name reached number one in the US and number two in the UK.

Gothic revival

A Goth grabbing a beer can to reveal her boulder-sized rings. Goth culture resurfaced in the late 1980s with emphasis upon customised leather jackets, pointed boots, black hats and lots of crushed velvet.

Tiananmen Square

Pro-democracy students in China march on Tiananmen Square in Beijing to join 150,000 other
protesters, demonstrating at the funeral of the sacked reformist politician, Hu Yao-Bang. The
demonstration was brutally suppressed as the army opened fire on the mainly unarmed protesters
killing several thousand people, which gained China widespread international condemnation.
Opposite: Greenham Women appeal to the Labour Party at the 1989 party conference. The United
States Air Base at Greenham became a site of controversy throughout the eighties as the US sited 96
cruise missiles there in 1981. Peace activists and feminists were constantly attracted to the cause during the decade. The missiles were not removed until 1991 following the collapse of the Soviet Union
and the end of the Cold War.

ACKNOWLEDGEMENTS

The photographs in this book are from the archives of the *Daily Mail*.
Particular thanks to Steve Torrington, Dave Sheppard, Brian Jackson, Alan Pinnock,
Richard Jones and all the staff.

Thanks also to Cliff Salter, Richard Betts, Gareth Thomas
Peter Wright, Trevor Bunting and Simon Taylor.
Design by John Dunne.